Friends Rule!

by Beth Mayall

SCHOLASTIC INC.
New York Toronto London Auckland Sydney
Mexico City New Delhi Hong Kong

ISBN 0-439-16103-7

12   4 5/0

Printed in the U.S.A.
First Scholastic printing, March 2000

Table of Contents

Friends Are the Best!

Friends are great. They are fun to be with, fun to laugh with, fun to have fun with. This book is all about you and your friends. In it you'll find:

- How to meet new friends.
- Tips on how to be a good friend.
- Fun activities and games to do with your friends.
- Plus, plenty of friendship puzzles!

Sometimes a hug says more than a million words.

Are you ready to be a good friend? Turn the page and find out!

Chapter One

Friends Are Easy to Find

If you look in the right places, it's easy to find girls who will make great friends. When you find someone you have something in common with, such as a hobby or a favorite book, you'll have a new friend and be having fun in no time!

A friend is someone who knows all about you . . . and loves you anyway!

If you like ...	then ...
singing	join the school chorus
reading	ask the girl who sits next to you about the book she's reading
sports	look for kids playing in your neighborhood and ask if you can join in
math	ask a classmate if she wants to do her homework with you
animals	talk to kids who walk dogs down your street
hiking	find out about the Girl Scouts
clothes	talk to a girl about the neat outfit she's wearing

Get-to-Know-You Games

Getting to know a new friend can be lots of fun! There are so many things to find out about — from her pets to her favorite stuffed animal to her worst dream ever. Here are some fun ways to get to know each other.

The Newspaper Game

Get a big sheet of poster board and turn it into a newspaper all about you and your friend. Interview each other about your families, your favorite subjects, anything you collect (like Beanie Babies or stickers). Write mini-stories, like "Christy Wins World Record for Eating the Most Pancakes!" or "The Mystery of the Missing Sneakers Solved!" Draw pictures or glue photos to the paper. Cut out pretty pictures from magazines and paste them onto the board. Then hang the newspaper up on your wall to enjoy every day!

Photo Album Mania!

Flip through each other's family photo albums and look at baby pictures of you and your friend. Share your favorite baby stories and ask your friend about her favorite memories.

Twenty-five Fun Questions

Ask each other this list of questions — some are deep and some are just plain kooky — and get to know each other a little bit better!

1. Are you ticklish?
2. What food do you love enough to eat every day?
3. What's your favorite pizza topping?
4. What do you want to be when you grow up?
5. What's your middle name?
6. What's your favorite color?

7. What do you like best about the way you look — your hair, your freckles, your nose, etc.?

8. What sport are you really good/great at?

9. If you could take a vacation anywhere in the world, where would you go?

10. Do you have any cousins?

11. Have you ever broken any bones?

12. What stuffed animal do you secretly love?

13. What do you most like to do with your family?

14. I'm happy when _____.

15. What's your favorite day of the week?

16. What three qualities do you look for in a friend?

17. What size shoes do you wear?

18. Is your belly button an innie or an outie?

19. What actor would you do backflips to meet right now?

20. What's your favorite book of all time?

21. If you could choose any movie to star in, which movie would you pick?
22. Do you know how to swim?
23. If you could be any animal for a day, which would you choose?
24. If you could get any gift right now, what would it be?
25. Would you rather dance, sing, act, or play an instrument in the school musical?

Help Out the New Girl

Have you ever moved to a new town or switched schools? If you have, then as the "new girl" you know you needed to discover how to find your class, where to sit at lunch, and how to talk to a new group of kids!

If you meet a new girl at school, you can help her feel welcome. You might even make a good friend! Here are some easy things to do:

1. Introduce her to your group of friends.
2. Invite her to have lunch with you and your friends.
3. Volunteer to show her all around school — the gym, the nurse's office, the playground, etc.
4. Lend her your class notes.
5. Ask her questions about her old school — Was it bigger or smaller? Did she ride the bus? Were the teachers nice? What was her old neighborhood or town like?

Five Ways to Talk to a New Girl in Your Class – or How to Make Friends with Anyone

Once you see someone who seems like she might be nice, try these five super conversation starters!

1. Look for something you'd really like to ask her about, such as:

"I love your jeans! Where did you get them?"

2. Are you interested in crafts such as jewelry making? Look for girls wearing handmade stuff and ask them if they made it, like:
"That's a neat friendship bracelet. Did you make it?"

3. Find out what someone is good at. If you know a girl who is great at math and you're having a hard time with that subject, she would probably love to help! Try this:
"Hey — can you help me with this math problem?"

4. Holidays are great because everyone gets excited about them and they are a great conversation starter, such as:
"I can't wait for Valentine's Day. What's your favorite kind of chocolate?"

5. If you notice someone who needs help, offer! Whether she's walking two dogs or cleaning erasers for the teacher, there are plenty of easy ways to be nice and helpful, as in: *"Can I help you with that?"*

All Kinds of Friends

Most of your friends are probably girls your age. But here are a few other kinds of friends that you can have lots of fun with.

1. *Who:* Younger friends, such as schoolmates in a grade or two below yours or little kids in your neighborhood.
What to do: Play games together, like tag or kick the can. Or practice a sport with them.
Why: It feels good to help someone learn something new!

2. *Who:* Older friends, such as kids a grade or two above you.

What to do: Hang out with them at lunch or after school.

Why: You'll get to meet a whole new group of friends and get to know what older kids talk about.

3. *Who:* Neighbors and the people on your street.

What to do: See if you can organize a group to play basketball or some other fun sport on the weekend. Or you could play video games together.

Why: It's cool to have an instant group of friends nearby, especially after school or on weekends.

4. *Who:* Relatives, such as aunts, uncles, cousins, grandparents, sisters, and brothers.

What to do: With older relatives, you can cook, sew, plant flowers, learn how to fix a car, and other fun stuff. With younger relatives, you can play games, have sleepover parties, and do crafts.

Why: You can learn how to do a lot of neat things. And your older relatives might have funny stories to share about what your parents were like when they were kids!

Here's a crossword to do with a friend. Have fun remembering songs from when you were little.

Sing-along Crossword Puzzle

Fill in the blanks with words from famous sing-along songs you probably sang when you were little! Find the answers on page 63.

ACROSS

1. There was a farmer who had a dog and _____ was his name, oh!

2. Take me out to the _____, take me out to the crowd! Buy me some peanuts and Cracker Jack . . .

3. If you're _____ and you know it, clap your hands.

4. Twinkle, twinkle, little star, how I _____ what you are.

DOWN

1. Row, row, row your _____.

2. I'm bringing home a _____ bumble-bee . . .

3. Do the _____ pokey . . .

5. I'm a little _____, short and stout . . .

6. _____ Doodle went to town . . .

7. _____ Bridge is falling down . . .

8. The itsy-bitsy _____ . . .

9. The _____ in the dell . . .

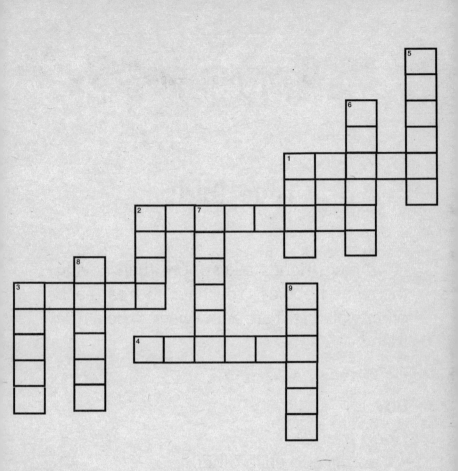

Chapter Two

True Buds

Being friends takes more than having the same hobbies. You have to treat each other well! Here are a few ways to be a true friend.

Do's

Good friends:
- are nice to each other.
- share their last piece of gum.
- spend time with each other.
- listen and help each other feel better when they're sad.
- are happy for each other.
- remember each other's birthdays.

- keep each other's secrets.
- let each other have other friends.

Don'ts
Good friends:
- don't ignore each other.
- don't call each other names, like ugly or fat.
- don't stay mad for very long.
- don't cancel plans with each other to go off and play with somebody else at the last minute.
- don't tell each other's secrets to other people.
- don't talk behind each other's backs.
- don't leave each other out when playing games.
- don't insist on always playing "my way."

Good friends
bring out the
best in you.

Friends Really Like Each Other

Good friends are like plants. They don't just appear overnight! Once you start a friendship, it takes a lot of care and attention to make it grow strong.

Friendships will blossom if you:

- *listen to each other.*
- *take turns doing what each one of you likes to do.*
- *treat each other like equals. One person cannot act like she's better than the other.*

Mini Quiz: Do You Choose Good Friends?

Place a check mark next to the statements that describe the way you feel about your friend.

___ **1.** I almost always have fun with her.
___ **2.** She has really good food at her house.

___ **3.** She isn't mean to people.

___ **4.** She's very popular, and that's important to me.

___ **5.** I can trust her.

___ **6.** If we fight, it takes her a long time before she will start talking to me again.

___ **7.** She doesn't make me feel bad about myself, like calling me dumb or ugly.

___ **8.** Sometimes I feel like I can't be myself around her.

___ **9.** She remembers things that are important to me, like my birthday.

___**10.** She has neat stuff I can use, like Rollerblades or a swimming pool.

If You Checked Mostly Odd-Numbered Statements (1, 3, 5, 7, 9): Hooray! You're definitely on the right track with this friend! She has all the qualities you should be looking for in a bud, which means she probably treats you well. Hold on to her!

If You Checked Mostly Even-Numbered Statements (2, 4, 6, 8, 10): Uh-oh! Looks like you'd better think again about this friend. For a friendship to last, you need to like a person's insides and she needs to like yours, too. Go back and read the odd-numbered statements to see if these qualities might matter more to you than how cool and popular your friend is.

It's Great to Have Lots of Different Friends

In every friendship, each person is good at certain things. For example, maybe you are great at Rollerblading and your friend is great at soccer. It's very important to be proud of your friend for the stuff she's great at! Good friends don't tease each other about not being good at something. (Instead, they help each other to improve!) Help your friend to be proud of her talents (and be sure she's proud of your abilities, too!).

Friendship Fill-in-the-Blanks

What is your best friend great at? What does she like to do? This fun exercise will help you learn more about each other.

On a separate sheet of paper, answer the following questions about your friend. Then have her answer the same questions about you on another sheet of paper. When you're done, trade papers to see what you wrote about each other.

1. Three words that describe my friend are _____, _____, and _____.
2. What I like best about my friend is _____.
3. She always makes me laugh when she _____.
4. I love her because _____ _____.
5. She is really good at _____ _____.
6. She has _____ brothers and sisters.

7. Her favorite kind of ice cream is _____

_____.

8. The song she loves most is _____

_____.

9. If she could pick a new name for herself, it would be _____.

10. Her favorite game to play is _____

_____.

Make a Pal Poem

How to do it: Write your friend's name on a sheet of paper with one letter on each line, like this:

K

E

R

R

I

Then come up with a word or phrase that starts with each letter of her name. The word should describe her personality or her talents in some way. For example:

Kind
Easy to talk to
Really funny
Reads lots of books
Incredible!

If you get stuck on a letter, here are a few suggestions to choose from:

A: Awesome
B: Beautiful
C: Cool
D: Dog lover
E: Excellent friend
F: Friendly
G: Good at sports
H: Happy
 I: Incredible
J: Just perfect
K: Knows how to listen
L: Laughs a lot

M: Makes people smile
N: Nice
O: Outstanding
P: Pretty
Q: Queen of soccer
R: Real friend
S: Smart
T: Terrific
U: Ultra-sweet
V: Very cool
W: Wild
X: X-cellent
Y: Year-round pal
Z: Zany

Girls Like You

We talked to girls like you! Here's what they had to say about what makes their friends special.

The neatest thing about my best friend is . . .

"Melissa can talk to anybody and not be

shy at all. I think that's neat." — Jenny,
California

"When I'm sad about something she'll
be at my side. She tickles me until I forget I
was sad!" — Leila, New York

"Even though my friend is a year older
than me (and a grade higher), she doesn't
act too cool for me. That means a lot to
me." — Meg, Pennsylvania

"Carrie got me interested in sports and
helped me figure out how much fun they
can be." — Nicole, Wisconsin

"My friend Jeannie wears whatever she
feels like wearing and she's nice to everybody at school. I think that's really
cool." — Teresa, Michigan

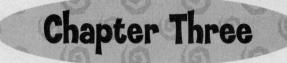

Chapter Three

Fun with Friends

Knowing someone who likes to do lots of the same things as you will add a million smiles to your day.

Here are some fun ideas.

Great Ideas for Fun at Home

- Teach your friend how to do something you know how to do, like twirl a baton or skate backward. Then let her teach you something she knows, like how to draw cartoons or do a cartwheel.

- Take the shoelaces out of each other's sneakers and print messages on them with colored laundry markers, then relace them.

- Have a special sleepover night! Invite your friend to spend the night at your house. You can "camp out" on the floor in sleeping bags and watch movies.

- Create new lyrics to your favorite song, using your nicknames and private jokes. Sing it into a tape recorder so you can listen to yourselves later.

- Make each other friendship rings with tiny beads. Take a twist tie, peel the coating off, and slip different colored beads onto the wire. Twist to close.

Make Funky, Lumpy Dough Dolls

Here's a fun project to do with a friend on a rainy day.

What You Need:
- A pot
- Metal spoon

- ½ cup cornstarch (plus a bit more)
- 1 cup baking soda
- ¼ cup and 2 tablespoons water
- Cookie sheet covered in waxed paper
- Paper towels
- Microwave oven
- Uncooked pasta (long noodles work best)
- Pencils
- Colored markers
- A grown-up's help

What You Do:

1. Have a grown-up pour the cornstarch, baking soda, and water into the pot, and stir with the metal spoon over medium-high heat on the stove top. The mixture will get foamy first, then thicken when it boils. When it gets thick, have the adult remove it from the heat and pour the mixture, which is now dough, onto the cookie sheet. Cover the dough with a wet paper towel.

2. Dust a countertop with extra corn-starch. Remove the paper towel and dump the dough onto the counter and keep mushing it around till it's smooth. (If it's too sticky, add more cornstarch.)

3. Divide the dough in half. One half is for you; the other half is for your friend.

4. Each of you should roll your dough into a ball.

5. Next, flatten the bottom so it sits upright on the waxed paper.

6. Turn the ball of dough into a model of your face! Make eyes and a mouth by poking deeply with a pencil (½ inch). Squeeze the "face" into your face shape. Pinch the dough into a nose. Make hair with uncooked pasta.

7. Pick up your sculptures on the waxed paper (leave the cookie sheet behind!) and have an adult slip them into the mi-crowave. Cook on high for 2 minutes, or until they're hard — it might take 30 seconds more. (Don't worry if they puff out.)

8. Let cool. Decorate your face a little with markers. When your creations are ready, trade so you have your friend's head and she has yours!

Good Reads for Good Friends

Check out these great, heart-warming books to share with your friends:

- The Ramona books by Beverly Cleary
- The Amber Brown books by Paula Danziger

COOL STUFF TO DO ALONE

It's okay if your friend is busy sometimes and can't play with you. Try some of these fun things when you have playtime by yourself.

- ◆ Surf the Net and check out fun Web sites for kids.
- ◆ Go for a walk or skip rope.
- ◆ Start a diary.
- ◆ Learn how to paint.
- ◆ Play a musical instrument.
- ◆ Stretch — it's really relaxing!
- ◆ Check out your basement or attic and see what cool, old stuff you can find.
- ◆ Memorize the lyrics to your favorite song.

- The Baby-sitters Little Sister books by Ann M. Martin
- The Little House books by Laura Ingalls Wilder
- The Harry Potter books by J. K. Rowling
- The Junie B. Jones books by Barbara Park
- The Pony Pals books by Jeanne Betancourt
- The American Girl books

Friendship Moments

Here are some quick tales from real girls about the times when friends helped them most.

"My best friend, Adrien, and I live right next door to each other. Before school sometimes she brings over a big mug of hot chocolate because she knows I hate to get up. It helps me get the day started with a smile." — Sissy, California

"My dog died last year, and Sarah let me cry on her shoulder until I felt better. She's one of the nicest people in the world." — Steph, Pennsylvania

SISTERS BY HEART
(a poem for my best friend, Tammy)
We have shared so much laughter
and shared many tears.
We have a special kinship
that grows stronger each year.
We are not sisters by birth,
but I knew it from the start
that fate put us together
to be sisters by heart.
— by Angela, Pennsylvania

Rainy Day Word Search

It's always fun on a rainy day to stay cozy indoors by playing board games with your friend. Here's a fun word search to get you in the mood. Find and circle each

of these fun board games in the puzzle below. The words can be found across, up,
down, and diagonally. Find the answers on
page 64.

Monopoly
Clue
Scrabble
Jenga
Uno
Sorry
Twister
Checkers
Mousetrap
Othello
Life

Friends are why
Reese's Peanut
Butter Cups
come in a
two-pack.

Y	C	W	V	J	S	M	M	B	L	K	Z	O
T	B	Q	A	X	E	O	L	J	Y	N	W	A
O	F	S	N	M	D	N	T	P	C	E	K	J
R	M	C	I	Z	A	O	G	H	H	F	Z	J
S	O	R	R	Y	H	P	Q	A	E	I	U	T
D	U	A	P	U	N	O	G	B	C	L	K	N
C	S	B	F	X	C	L	U	E	K	R	L	I
V	E	B	D	I	L	Y	C	H	E	M	R	O
C	T	L	T	W	I	S	T	E	R	E	S	A
E	R	E	W	D	S	E	J	F	S	X	O	U
Q	A	T	B	P	V	O	H	K	G	H	I	L
U	P	R	G	G	F	E	D	Y	N	Z	E	F

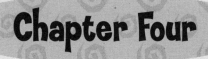

Chapter Four

Bad Times with Good Friends

Nobody likes to fight. But you and your friend might not always get along. Don't worry — this happens to all friends! But if you work through it, you could end up closer than ever before.

What We Fight About Most

Here are what some friends argue about:

1."I feel left out."

If your friend suddenly starts spending less time with you (and more time with somebody else!) it hurts.

The truth: It's good for people to have more than one close friend, so try not to be too hurt if your friend is close with someone else, too.

How to fix the ouch: When your friend is busy, go hang out with someone you'd like to get to know better. Soon you'll have a group of friends, too, and it won't hurt so much. Another idea: Ask your friend if you and her other pal can all play together. Try to find something in common with your bud's other friend. Maybe you'll find you really like each other.

2. "No fair!"

Maybe your friend always wants to choose the movie. Or she always asks you to come to her house on the weekend, but she never comes to your house.

The truth: She might not realize she's being unfair.

How to fix the ouch: Friendship is about compromise. If you feel like it's your turn, say so. Try this: "We spent last

Saturday at your house, so can you come to my house this Saturday?"

3. "Don't call me that!"

A little teasing is usually okay between friends, but sometimes jokes can hurt.

The truth: Everybody's sensitive about something. (You probably are, too.)

How to fix the ouch: Is your best friend touchy about her grades? Her big feet? Her braces? Respect her limits and don't tease her about it.

4. "You're not the boss of me!"

Sometimes one friend will make all the decisions: what games to play, where to go, and so on.

The truth: When this happens, someone's usually just trying to come up with something fun to do and doesn't realize she's being bossy.

How to fix the ouch: If you're the bossy one, apologize and ask your friend what she'd like to do instead. If you're being bossed around, suggest something you'd like to do instead.

Fighting Do's and Don'ts

Do . . . say how you feel.

Don't . . . call your friend bad names, like "brat" or "bossy."

Do . . . listen to what your friend says.

Don't . . . yell! When you both yell, nobody is listening.

Do . . . stick to the point of what made you angry. For example, "I felt left out when you didn't call me back on Friday."

Don't . . . use phrases like "You ALWAYS" or "You NEVER." You shouldn't bring up old fights if you want to resolve the new one.

Do . . . say what's on your mind. You can't fix the fight if you're afraid to let her know what you think she did wrong.

Don't . . . say things you don't mean, like "I hate you!" or "I don't want to be friends anymore!" Those things can leave hard feelings and can be tough to take back.

Word Scramble-up!

Below is a list of five scrambled words. Unscramble each of them and figure out which of these five things you would NOT find in your friend's bedroom! Find the answers on page 65.

1. IRYAD
2. ESSHO
3. HESOLCT
4. KOBOS
5. ZIAPZ

A true friend
is always
ready to
lend a hand.

Sometimes Friendships End

There are some friends you'll be close with for a long time. And there are others who you'll be close with for a while, but the friendship won't last forever. It happens to everyone. Here are some of the most common reasons that friendships fade:

- *You become interested in different things.* If you used to play soccer together and now you're into ballet instead, you might spend less time with each other.
- *You meet new people.* If a friendship blossoms between you and a new friend, it could make you drift away from your old friend.
- *You move or change schools.* If you suddenly don't see your friend as frequently, it could hurt your friendship.

How to Stay Friends Even When You're Miles Apart

Listen to these girls' secrets for staying close with friends who live far away:

"When my best friend Alicia moved to Arizona, I thought I might die! We both cried the whole week before she left. But now we e-mail each other every day and sometimes we get on-line at the same time so we can type instant messages back and forth." — Catherine, Georgia

"I moved six hours away from my friend Maria, but we're still close! We spent the whole summer together — three weeks at my house, then three weeks at her house. During the school year we talk on the phone once a week and send letters to each other." — Amelia, Texas

"Last year, my family and I moved away from the Philippines to Canada. It

hurts being away from my friend Rica, but we write letters and send voice tapes to each other. That's how we stay close."
— Michelle, Ontario, Canada

"My friend and I used to bake cookies together all the time, before she had to move with her family. So now whenever I miss her, I'll have my mom help me bake cookies and send them to her in the mail. Sometimes she sends me brownies or Rice Krispie treats. It's a nice surprise!"
— Bonnie, Oklahoma

Here's a recipe Bonnie recommends.

Bonnie's Peanut-Butter Cookies

What You Need:

- 1 cup peanut butter (creamy or chunky)
- 1 cup sugar
- 1 large egg
- A grown-up to help you

- Cookie sheet
- Mixing bowls
- Mixing spoon
- Metal spatula
- Metal baking rack

What You Do:

1. Have an adult preheat the oven to 350°F.
2. Combine the ingredients in a bowl and stir until well mixed.
3. Drop the dough by teaspoonfuls onto the cookie sheet, about 1 inch apart.
4. Have an adult bake the cookies on the middle oven rack for 8 minutes.
5. Let cool slightly, then have an adult use a metal spatula to move the cookies to the baking rack to cool completely.

Chapter Five

Hands-on Fun

Here are some neat activities for you and your friends to enjoy together.

Face Painting

What You Need:

- 6 teaspoons cornstarch
- 3 teaspoons water
- 3 teaspoons cold cream
- Food coloring
- 6-cup muffin tin (or six small dishes)

What You Do:

1. Put 1 teaspoon cornstarch and a ½ teaspoon each of cold cream and water in each cup of the muffin tin.

2. Add a different food coloring to each cup and mix well. There! Your paints are ready.

3. Take turns painting each other's faces. (The paint will wash off easily.) Be careful not to get paint in your friend's eyes or mouth!

Super-duper String Sculpture

What You Need:
- A balloon
- Glue
- A paper plate
- Lots of string
- Food coloring or glitter (optional)

What You Do:

1. Blow up the balloon and knot it.
2. Pour glue onto the paper plate. (You can also put glitter or food coloring in the glue to make the string fancy!)
3. Dip a long piece of string into the glue,

then wrap it around the balloon. Keep dipping and wrapping until you like the pattern you've created with the string.

4. When you're done, tie a string to the knot of the balloon and hang it upside down to dry for a few days.

5. When it's dry, pop the balloon and re-move the broken pieces. The string will stay in the shape of the balloon and you'll have a Super-duper String Sculpture!

Jazzy Jar

What You Need:
- A jar (a small one, like a baby-food jar)
- Bright crayons
- Scissors
- Aluminum foil
- A pretty piece of ribbon
- A hot, sunny day!

What You Do:

1. Pick three different crayons and have a grown-up cut them into small pieces with the scissors for you. (If you use a bigger jar, you will need more crayons.)
2. Unwrap the crayon pieces.
3. Go outside and place the foil on the ground in a hot, sunny area. Put the cut-up crayon pieces on the foil. They will melt quickly!
4. When the crayons are mostly melted but still lumpy, quickly roll your jar around in the colors until you like the design. (Note: Don't wait for the crayons to melt completely, or they will turn into one ugly color!)
5. Take the jar to a cool place to harden, then tie a bow around the top of the jar with your ribbon! Note: Keep the jar out of bright sunlight and away from heat or the crayon will melt off!

Friendship Shirts

What You Need:
- 2 plain white T-shirts
- Crayons
- Paper towels
- An iron and ironing board
- A grown-up's supervision

What You Do:

1. Draw or write on the front of the T-shirt with crayons. Make your lines bold and thick. If you draw a character or image (flower, face, whatever cute thing you imagine), make sure it's completely filled in — it transfers better that way!

2. Cover the image with paper towels. Also place paper towels INSIDE the shirt, covering the entire space you colored.

3. Have a grown-up set the iron on high and iron over the paper towels several times until the colors are bright and the fabric is soft.

4. Remove the paper towels and give the shirt to your friend! (To keep the shirt looking its best, it should be hand-washed and line-dried.)

Friendship Scrapbook

What You Need:
- Empty binder with pockets
- A bunch of sheets of looseleaf paper
- Glue stick
- Scissors
- Old magazines that you can cut up
- Colored markers
- Stickers
- Photos of you and your friend

What You Do:

1. With your friend, go through the magazines and cut out words and pictures that you like. Glue them onto the front, back, and spine of the binder to make an offi-

cial friendship album! (Be sure to cover every blank space!)

2. Put the looseleaf paper in the binder.
3. Write about your favorite places to hang out, your favorite TV shows, your favorite stores in the mall, whatever!
4. Glue in the photos of you and your friend. Write down where you were and mention anything special that happened on the day the photo was taken.
5. Include ticket stubs, stickers, tiny souvenirs, cutouts of shopping bags from your favorite stores — anything you can glue down that reminds you of your times together.
6. Decorate all the pages with markers and stickers.
7. Ta-da! Put your album away and look at it anytime you're together and don't know what to do. Add pages and stuff as your friendship grows!

"Fun Stuff" Word Search

Find and circle each of these fun-related words in the puzzle below. The answers are on page 66.

Run
Jump
Play
Hide
Ride
Skip
Laugh
Sing
Dance
Skate
Walk
Yell
Talk
Call
Share
Hug
Care
Give
Race
Write

Friends can turn a rainy afternoon into the best time ever.

L	G	I	V	E	L	R	E	E	Q	O	P	D	W
R	M	U	M	A	K	D	A	D	D	T	R	E	R
A	Y	E	L	L	I	E	B	W	B	A	C	A	I
C	O	A	L	H	T	A	G	Q	C	L	N	S	T
E	A	S	J	A	N	U	N	P	J	K	B	C	E
N	I	E	K	B	H	O	L	A	U	G	H	O	E
O	F	S	G	I	K	E	O	U	M	D	H	C	T
C	A	R	E	D	P	W	J	I	P	I	G	R	V
A	W	Y	R	J	V	A	A	N	D	N	U	J	E
S	D	H	I	U	E	L	H	K	I	S	F	L	N
E	H	E	D	C	N	K	E	S	I	L	L	O	K
X	F	A	E	N	L	M	A	P	L	A	Y	E	A
U	F	U	R	I	G	Y	F	O	C	U	G	R	T
I	G	E	O	E	N	I	E	M	E	U	L	L	H

the best. Answers are on page

Chapter Six

Friendship Fun for More Than One

Two of a Kind Fill-in-the-Blanks

Finish these common phrases. Hint: They're all about things that go together (like best friends). Answers are on page 67.

1. Cake and _____ _____
2. Barbie and _____
3. ____ and cookies
4. Hot _____ and marshmallows
5. _____ _____ and jelly

Pigpen

A game to play with a friend.

What You Need:
- Paper
- Two pencils

What You Do:

1. Make a grid of dots, four along each side, like this:

```
.   .   .   .

.   .   .   .

.   .   .   .

.   .   .   .
```

2. Take turns connecting two dots. You cannot connect dots diagonally, only up and down or side to side.

3. When you form a box, write your initial in the box and take another turn. The person with the most boxes at the end wins.

Magical Memory Game

A game to play with one or more friends.

What You Need:
• A deck of playing cards

What You Do:

1. Shuffle the cards.
2. Lay all the cards facedown on a table in rows.
3. Choose two cards.
4. If they match (for example, two sevens or two queens), put them in a pile and choose two more. If they do not match, return them to their places facedown. Try to remember where the cards are so you can pick up pairs as the game continues.

5. Then it is the next player's turn. You will keep taking turns until all the cards are gone. The player with the most cards at the end wins!

Ticktock Word Search

A word search contest between you and your friend! Find the answers on pages 68–69.

What You Need:
• Two pens or pencils

What You Do:

1. Find and circle the following list of words in your puzzle. (They are hidden in different places, so it doesn't matter if you see each other's puzzles.)
2. Whoever finds all the words first wins!

FOR LEFT-HAND PAGE
Player One: Find These Words:

Red
Yellow

Pink
Green
Purple
Orange
Blue
White
Black
Gray

R	E	W	U	P	D	E	P	G	R	K	I	D	Q	W	A	E
U	G	O	Z	R	U	H	N	B	E	Y	P	E	W	T	X	F
G	R	A	Y	A	G	R	I	A	D	T	L	A	D	R	T	B
B	A	G	M	L	M	A	P	P	E	N	I	H	O	U	X	L
O	D	Q	G	V	E	L	B	L	A	C	K	D	E	G	E	U
U	A	N	R	E	K	S	Y	A	E	Y	R	T	Y	A	M	E
L	J	Y	E	L	L	O	W	E	N	T	I	I	C	E	H	E
P	N	R	E	L	R	Z	N	N	K	H	B	R	E	P	O	R
R	E	A	N	A	E	F	O	T	W	J	O	N	P	W	D	L
I	R	U	N	B	D	E	G	R	P	U	G	E	L	I	V	E
E	L	G	Y	U	S	K	E	Y	I	L	A	C	U	P	N	B
P	E	L	N	L	E	N	A	L	D	U	R	I	O	L	O	K

Player Two: Find These Words:

Red
Yellow
Pink
Green
Purple
Orange
Blue
White
Black
Gray

My Grandmother's Suitcase

A game to play with one or more friends.

What You Do:

1. One person starts the game by saying, "I packed my grandmother's suitcase and in it I packed . . ." She finishes the sentence with a word that starts with the letter A. (It can be anything — even something weird, like Astronaut!)
2. The second player repeats the phrase, "I packed my grandmother's suitcase and in it I packed . . ." She will repeat the A word and come up with an item that starts with a B to add to the list.
3. Go back and forth through the alphabet, repeating the list until someone forgets one of the items!

Sample: "I packed my grandmother's suitcase and in it I packed . . . an Astronaut, a Blanket, a Candy bar, a Dragon, an Elephant . . ." all the way to the letter Z!

First and Last

A game to play with one or more friends.

What You Do:

1. Choose a category you know well, like animals or food or items in your room.
2. The first player says a word in that category. Then the next player says a word in that category that begins with the last letter of that word. For example: The topic is "food." The first player says "sandwich." Player two must come up with a food word that starts with the letter H (the last

letter in *sandwich*), so you could say "hamburger" (or some other H word).

3. The next player must then come up with a food word that starts with R, which is the last letter in *hamburger*.
4. The game ends when one player can't think of a word in that category and the other player can — and becomes the winner. Then you start over with a new category.

Straw Soccer

A game to play with one or more friends.

What You Need:
• Drinking straws
• A Ping-Pong ball (or a piece of paper crumpled to that size)
• A ruler
• Masking tape

What You Do:

1. On a smooth table or floor, create a "playing field" using the ruler and masking tape. The play zone should be about 2 feet wide and 3 feet long.
2. Mark a goal for each player with more masking tape. It should be about 6 inches long.
3. Drop the ball (or crumpled paper) in the middle of the playing field.
4. Each player blows through her straw to make the ball go through the other player's goal.
5. Whoever gets 10 goals first wins!

Conclusion

Friends Rule

Friendships are kind of like roller skating. Sometimes the road is smooth (whee!) and sometimes it's bumpy and tough. You go up and down hills and sometimes you fall and scrape your knee. But usually you have a fun ride.

In this book hopefully you have learned ways to help you make new friends and keep old buds. Use them! You could end up with the best friends you've ever had.

Friendship Answer Key

Chapter One

Answers to Sing-along Crossword Puzzle (pages 12–13)

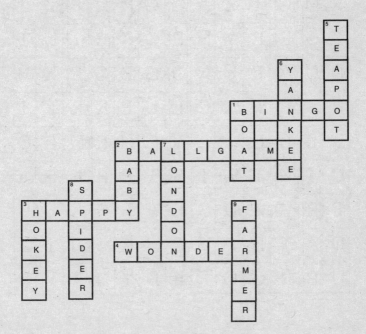

Chapter Three

Answers to Rainy Day Word Search (pages 32–33)

Y	C	W	V	J	S	M	M	B	L	K	Z	O
T	B	Q	A	X	E	O	L	J	Y	N	W	A
O	F	S	N	M	D	N	T	P	C	E	K	J
R	M	C	I	Z	A	O	G	H	H	F	Z	J
S	O	R	R	Y	H	P	Q	A	E	I	U	T
D	U	A	P	U	N	O	G	B	C	L	K	N
C	S	B	F	X	C	L	U	E	K	R	L	I
V	E	B	D	I	L	Y	C	H	E	M	R	O
C	T	L	T	W	I	S	T	E	R	E	S	A
E	R	E	W	D	S	E	J	F	S	X	O	U
Q	A	T	B	P	V	O	H	K	G	H	I	L
U	P	R	G	G	F	E	D	Y	N	Z	E	F

Chapter Four

Answers to Word Scramble-up! (page 37)

1. Diary
2. Shoes
3. Clothes
4. Books
5. Pizza (This is the one you wouldn't find in her room.)

Chapter Five

Answers to "Fun Stuff" Word Search (pages 49–50)

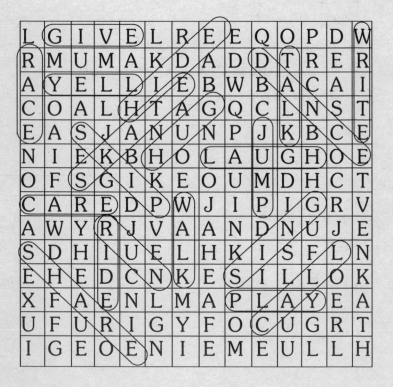

Chapter Six

Answers to Two of a Kind Fill-in-the-Blanks
(page 51)

1. Ice cream
2. Ken
3. Milk
4. Chocolate
5. Peanut butter

Answers to Ticktock Word Search (pages 54–56)

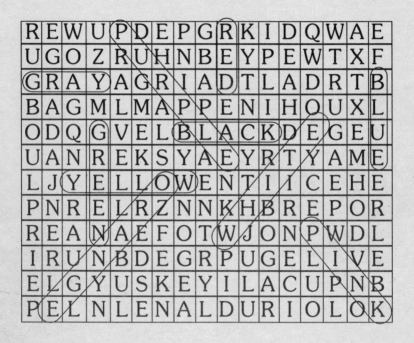

R	E	W	U	P	D	E	P	G	R	K	I	D	Q	W	A	E
U	G	O	Z	R	U	H	N	B	E	Y	P	E	W	T	X	F
G	R	A	Y	A	G	R	I	A	D	T	L	A	D	R	T	B
B	A	G	M	L	M	A	P	P	E	N	I	H	O	U	X	L
O	D	Q	G	V	E	L	B	L	A	C	K	D	E	G	E	U
U	A	N	R	E	K	S	Y	A	E	Y	R	T	Y	A	M	E
L	J	Y	E	L	L	O	W	E	N	T	I	I	C	E	H	E
P	N	R	E	L	R	Z	N	N	K	H	B	R	E	P	O	R
R	E	A	N	A	E	F	O	T	W	J	O	N	P	W	D	L
I	R	U	N	B	D	E	G	R	P	U	G	E	L	I	V	E
E	L	G	Y	U	S	K	E	Y	I	L	A	C	U	P	N	B
P	E	L	N	L	E	N	A	L	D	U	R	I	O	L	O	K

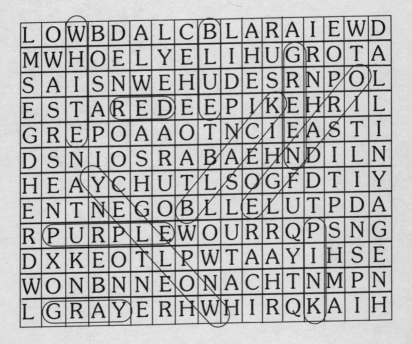

L	O	W	B	D	A	L	C	B	L	A	R	A	I	E	W	D
M	W	H	O	E	L	Y	E	L	I	H	U	G	R	O	T	A
S	A	I	S	N	W	E	H	U	D	E	S	R	N	P	O	L
E	S	T	A	R	E	D	E	E	P	I	K	E	H	R	I	L
G	R	E	P	O	A	A	O	T	N	C	I	E	A	S	T	I
D	S	N	I	O	S	R	A	B	A	E	H	N	D	I	L	N
H	E	A	Y	C	H	U	T	L	S	O	G	F	D	T	I	Y
E	N	T	N	E	G	O	B	L	L	E	L	U	T	P	D	A
R	P	U	R	P	L	E	W	O	U	R	R	Q	P	S	N	G
D	X	K	E	O	T	L	P	W	T	A	A	Y	I	H	S	E
W	O	N	B	N	N	E	O	N	A	C	H	T	N	M	P	N
L	G	R	A	Y	E	R	H	W	H	I	R	Q	K	A	I	H